First published in Great Britain 1984 by
Hamish Hamilton Children's Books
Garden House, 57–59 Long Acre, London WC2E 9JZ

British Library Cataloguing in Publication Data

Snell, Nigel
Sue learns to cross the road
1. Traffic safety – Juvenile literature
I Title
363.1'2575 HE5614
ISBN 0-241-11299-0 (hardback)
ISBN 0-241-11463-2 (paperback)

Printed in Great Britain by
Cambus Litho, East Kilbride

Sue Learns to Cross the Road

NIGEL SNELL

Hamish Hamilton · London

Mummy and Sue were going shopping.
They were walking along a busy road.
Lots of cars, buses and lorries
drove past them.

Sue had her pet alligator with her.
Of course, he was not a real alligator,
but he did frighten people a bit!

AT NIGHT WEAR WHITE
GO

Ahead of them they could see
some children playing.
One boy was chasing the others.
They were all laughing and shouting.

Suddenly, another boy ran out into the road.
A big lorry was coming.
The driver had to brake very hard.

NIG 1 L
SCREECH
SCREECH

The boy only just got out of the way.
He was lucky not to be knocked down.
The lorry driver shouted at him,
'You should learn to cross
the road properly.'
He was very cross.

‘What a silly boy!’ said Mummy.
‘He could have been badly hurt,
or even killed.
Make sure you never cross the road
without looking.
Watch me, and I’ll show you what to do.’

When they got to the next road,
Mummy told Sue to wait at the kerb.

'Always try to cross where you can
see the road clearly both ways.
And make sure motorists can see you.

‘Then look both ways and listen carefully.
Even if you can’t see anything,
there might be a car coming round the corner.

‘If the road is clear, and
there is no sound of any traffic,
walk across the road.
Don’t run!

'Try not to cross between parked cars.
But if you have to, make sure
there is no-one inside them.
If a car started to move,
you might be trapped.'

30

Sue looked both ways and listened carefully.
When she was sure it was safe to cross,
she took Mummy's hand and
walked quickly to the other side.

'We will buy you a reflector belt,' said Mummy.
'Then motorists will be able to see you better when it is dark or wet.
The orange glow of the belt will warn them that you are there.

And we will get the Green Cross Code book.
Then you will always remember how to cross the road.'

Sue was very pleased.
How smart the belt would look.

But what about her alligator?
His tail stuck out such a long way
cars might easily run over it.
Couldn't he have a reflector belt too?
Mummy nodded, and sighed.

SQUELCH
SQUELCH

The End